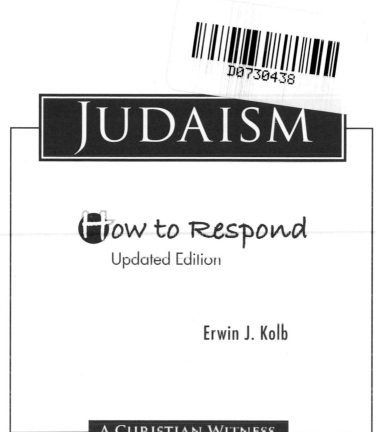

JUDAISM

How to Respond
Updated Edition

Erwin J. Kolb

A CHRISTIAN WITNESS

CONCORDIA PUBLISHING HOUSE · SAINT LOUIS

This edition published 2010 Concordia Publishing House.
Text copyright © 1990, 1995 Concordia Publishing House.
3558 S. Jefferson Avenue, St. Louis, MO 63118–3968

1-800-325-3040 • www.cph.org

Originally published as *How to Respond to Judaism* in The Response Series © 1990 Concordia Publishing House.

Scripture quotations are from the ESV Bible® (The Holy Bible, English Standard Version®), copyright © 2010 by Crossway Bibles, a publishing ministry of Good News Publishers. Used by permission. All rights reserved.

Manufactured in the United States of America

Library of Congress Cataloging-in-Publication Data

Kolb, Erwin J.
   Judaism / Erwin J. Kolb. —Rev. ed.
p. cm.   —(How to respond series)
   Rev. ed. of: How to respond to . . . Judaism © 1990.
   Includes bibliographical references.
   ISBN 0-7586-1628-7

   1. Judaism. 2. Missions to Jews. 3. Christianity and other religions—Judaism—1945- 4. Judaism—Relations—Christianity—1945- I. Kolb, Erwin J. How to respond to—Judaism. II. Title. III. Series.

   BV2620.K6 1995
   261.2'6—dc20   95–450

1 2 3 4 5 6 7 8 9 10   19 18 17 16 15 14 13 12 11 10

CONTENTS

1 A New Spirit

As I grew up in a Lutheran community in Bay City, Michigan, I did not personally know any Jewish people. The only Jews I heard about were those in the Bible—the nasty ones who opposed Jesus and plotted His death, and the good ones who followed Him. Today most of the Michigan Christians I talk to do know some Jews, hear a lot about them in the media, and have definite opinions about them.

There is a new awareness of the Jewish people today and a new spirit of concern about them. Jews are visible and vocal, and their numbers have increased, though they make up only 2.3 percent of the United States' population. Who does not know the names of prominent Jewish contemporaries such as statesmen Henry Kissinger and Rahm Emmanuel; scientists Albert Einstein and Jonas Salk; astronaut Judith Resnik; theologians Abraham Heschel and Elie Wiesel; violinist Jascha Heifetz; pianists Vladimir Horowitz and Arthur Rubinstein; composers Leonard

Bernstein, Irving Berlin, and George Gershwin; performers Victor Borge, Bob Dylan, Jack Benny, Barbara Streisand, and Paul Newman; movie director Steven Spielberg; and many others.

The number of Jews in America has increased roughly like this:

1776   2,000

1820   4,000

1880   280,000

1925   4,500,000

1992   5,800,000

2006   5,200,000

The quoted figures of the number of Jewish people in the United States or the world varies from source to source. The Council of Jewish Federations says there are 6.8 million Jews in the United States. The *Yearbook of American and Canadian Churches* lists 5.9 million Jews. The Center for Cultural Judaism reissued a study "American Jewish Identity Survey" (2001) that lists 5.3 million Jews in America. The states with the largest number of Jews, in order, are New York, California, Florida, and Pennsylvania. There are approximately 12.9 million Jewish people in the world.[1]

JEWISH AGGRESSIVENESS

As the American Jewish population increased, they became more visible and influential in many areas of American society. The Jewish community has become more organized, locally and nationally, in order to promote Jewish causes, oppose anti-Semitism, and most recently to seek support for the nation of Israel. In a pamphlet authored by Peter Y. Medding, the American Jewish Committee lists two of its priorities as the security of Israel and the welfare of Soviet Jews.[2]

In that pamphlet, Medding writes that Jewish Americans believe they must defend their status in American society against "two major hostile pressures": (1) the threat of anti-Semitic prejudice and discrimination and (2) the threat of the incorporation of Christian symbols, practices, and values into public life. Because of the past history of persecution and repeated attempts at annihilation, as in the Holocaust, American Jews suffer, he says, from a "permanent sense of insecurity and vulnerability."

As a result of this new spirit among American Jews as well as the rise of secular humanism (a philosophy seeking to enable humans to live fulfilling lives apart from belief in God), one reads almost daily of efforts to eliminate the cross from public buildings. Recent years have seen an increase in efforts to remove Christmas carols and programs from public schools and manger scenes from public property. Religious News Service reported in August 1989 that a federal judge ordered the removal of a Latin cross that had been displayed atop a municipal water tower in St. Cloud, Florida, for more than twenty years because it was a symbol of Christianity. U.S. District Judge G. Kendall Sharp said that no federal court has allowed a Latin cross to remain on government property because "it is an obvious perception of Christianity to any persons of non-Christian faith." The complaint was made by a Jewish resident of St. Cloud who said that the cross reminded him of relatives who died during the Holocaust. The ACLU (American Civil Liberties Union) assisted the protester in the legal process.

Oddly, the judge ruled that St. Cloud could replace the Latin cross with a Greek cross because that was more neutral and was not perceived as a Christian symbol. This, too, was challenged, but the city dropped the issue because of the tremendous legal costs.

8

Yes, there is a new spirit abroad in the *goy* (Gentile) community and in the Jewish community. Jews have begun to exert their views with more *chutzpah* (a Yiddish expression for "unmitigated nerve"). They press for toleration, emphasizing that in our pluralistic society no specific religion can be considered better than another, and that no one religion can be proclaimed as the "true" religion while another is proclaimed to be "false." Jews insist that to say Judaism is false is prejudiced and anti-Semitic.

THE RESPONSE TO JEWISH AGGRESSIVENESS

Unfortunately, one of the ways in which people have responded to the new aggressiveness of the Jewish community is with an increase in anti-Semitism. In 1989, according to Abraham Fox of the Anti-Defamation League, there were fourteen hundred anti-Semitic incidents against Jewish institutions and property, the highest in eleven years of counting the incidents. Recently, however, the Anti-Defamation League reported that overall incidents have decreased over the last four years with 1,352 incidents occurring in 2008.

The increase in anti-Semitism is worldwide. In Japan, where there is only a small number of Jews, eighty anti-Semitic books were published in a one-year period, according to Mr. Fox. In Germany, resentment against Jews is growing. In Israel, in response to the rise in attacks on Jews all over the world, the Israeli Cabinet called on "democratic and anti-racist forces" in all the countries of the world "to mobilize for action against manifestations of anti-Semitism."

One of the ways in which the church has reacted to this new spirit is to retreat from the biblical principle that clearly states that the Gospel of Jesus Christ is for Jew and Gentile. "I am not ashamed of the gospel, for it is the power of God for salvation to everyone who believes, to the Jew first and also to the Greek" (Romans 1:16).

The director of the Anti-Defamation League of B'nai B'rith reports that anti-Semitism today is more ugly and dangerous than in previous times because the basis is shifting from social and religious to *political.* In fact, the director also stated that some in the United States blamed Jews for the attacks on 9/11 (Anti-Defamation League, "ADL Says U.S. Based Anti-Semites are Feeding Sept. 11 Rumor Mill," news release, November 9, 2001).

In preparation for a presentation to the Lausanne Consultation on Jewish Evangelism in 1978, I surveyed fifty major denominations in the United States regarding their positions and outreach activities to Jewish people. Only half of the denominations responded. Among them only a few of the more evangelical and conservative denominations were involved in Jewish evangelism. Most of the denominations were struggling to harmonize the traditional biblical view and a more "modern" and "tolerant" view that sought to espouse a "two covenant" theory. The two-covenant approach, which is precisely what some Jewish people have maintained since the time of Christ, claims that the Mosaic covenant is for Jews and the covenant established by Jesus is for Christians. Both, it is said, are valid ways to salvation. This kind of thinking results in positions like the one expressed by Eric W. Gritsch in a booklet published by The Lutheran Council, USA: "There really is no need for any Christian mission to the Jews. They are and remain the people of God, even if they do not accept Jesus as their Messiah."[3] The Lutheran World Federation stated, "We affirm the integrity of our two faith communities and repudiate any organized proselyting of each other."

Apparently some modern-day disciples of Jesus Christ have forgotten the teaching of their Lord: "I am the way, the truth, and the life. No one comes to the Father except through Me" (John 14:6). The modern Church, it seems, no longer remembers the teaching of the Early Church: "And there is salvation in no one else, for there is no other name [other than the name of Jesus Christ] under heaven

given among men by which we must be saved"
(Acts 4:12).

THE CHALLENGE TO SHARE THE GOSPEL

Meanwhile the challenge and opportunity to share the
Gospel with the Jewish people continues to grow. Gallup
reports that in all of his findings, Jews are less religious
than other Americans. Of Jewish Americans, 44 percent
say they are members of a synagogue, compared with
69 percent of the general population who claim membership in a church or synagogue. Of Jews attending
synagogue, 21 percent reported attending synagogue
the week of the survey, compared to 40 percent of the
general population. Of Jewish Americans, 35 percent
said religion is "not very important" in their lives, compared with 14 percent of all Americans.

The Lutheran Church—Missouri Synod (LCMS) also
responded to the new spirit, but differently than most
other church bodies, in a way consistent with its history
of concern for sharing the Gospel with Jewish people.
Already in 1881, the Central District of the Missouri
Synod petitioned the Church "to consider its responsibility
for establishing a synodical means of enlisting and coor-
dinating the interest and obligation of every Christian to
bear witness to his Jewish fellowmen." In 1884, the Synod

established a *Kommission fur Judenmission* (Commission for Jewish Mission) that functioned until 1932, when the Synod turned over the responsibility for Jewish evangelism to its districts. But little was done by the districts.

Some metropolitan areas during this time called full-time missionaries to Jewish people:

New York   1883–1941

Chicago   1930–1939

St. Louis   1930–1934

In 1972, an LCMS congregation in the Philadelphia area, St. Luke's Lutheran Church, became concerned for the Jewish people and sent a memorial (a proposed resolution) for consideration at the Church's national convention:

> *Resolved*, That the Synod instruct the District Boards for Evangelism to focus their attention on the task of bringing the Gospel of the atonement through faith in Jesus Christ as the promised Messiah to the Jewish people; and be it further

> *Resolved*, That the Synod's Board for Evangelism produce guidelines and materials which will aid individuals, congregations, and districts in this effort.

This resolution was referred to the national Board for Evangelism to implement. They did so by appointing a special Committee for Witnessing to Jewish People, which continues to function today as the Task Force for Witnessing to Jewish People. Since national convention in 1972, the LCMS has passed several supporting resolutions restating its concern to share with Jewish people that Jesus is the Messiah. The Committee for Witnessing to Jewish People responded by producing material to help congregations and individuals understand the beliefs and traditions of Judaism and witness with love to Jewish people. This work continues in the organization, The Apple of His Eye (AOHE) Mission Society, which resulted from cooperation between the LCMS World Mission and the Missouri District of the LCMS.[4]

2 WHAT IS JUDAISM?

Bruce Lieske, the author of *Witnessing to Jewish People*, a manual produced by The Lutheran Church—Missouri Synod's Task Force on Witnessing to Jewish People, tells the story of a Christian woman who, out of curiosity, attended a synagogue service. After the service she visited with the rabbi. As he encouraged her to ask questions, she inquired, "Where do you keep the sheep and other animals for the sacrifices?" As ludicrous as this sounds, it illustrates the many ways Christians perceive Judaism. Their perceptions are based on their knowledge of the Bible, Old Testament temple worship, and Jesus' dealings with the scribes and Pharisees of His day.

To understand Judaism today, one must clearly distinguish between the faith of the Old Testament, called biblical Judaism, and modern Judaism, known as rabbinic or Talmudic Judaism. It is rabbinic if its source is the teachings of the rabbis, or Talmudic if its source is the Talmud. Jews have traditionally considered the Talmud, an eighteen-volume set of rabbinical teachings written from about AD 200 to 600, the authoritative commentary on the Old Testament Scriptures. Judaism traditionally has taught that the content of the Talmud was given orally by God to Moses on Mount Sinai and then passed on by mouth until it was written down.

Judaism is the religion of the Jewish people. The ethnic ancestors of the Jews are the Hebrews, or the Israelites. The origins of the Jewish race began when God called Abraham (Genesis 12:1–3) and entered into a covenant with him, promising to make a "special" people of his descendants. God established the line of descent through Isaac and Jacob (Israel). Under the leadership of Moses, God created a unique way of life for His chosen people. He centered their worship in the tabernacle, which was replaced under Solomon with the temple. God gave specific regulations for a system of offerings, sacrifices, diet, keeping the Sabbath, and almost every aspect of life, including the reading of the Torah (the five books of Moses). Through this special people God promised to send a Messiah who would redeem the world by His suffering, death, and resurrection.

When the Babylonians destroyed the first temple in 587 BC and took most of the remaining Israelites in Judah to

Babylon, God taught His people, through the prophets Ezekiel and Daniel, to worship without sacrifices. They focused instead on the reading of Scripture and prayer, and thus the synagogue began to develop. However, the Israelites returned, rebuilt the temple, and continued the sacrificial system for almost six hundred more years. After the close of the Old Testament period (about 400 BC), the faith of the Israelites changed and Judaism emerged. It is proper to call God's people in the Old Testament "Israelites" or "Hebrews" (descendants of Abraham through Isaac and Jacob, or Israel), while reserving "Jews" for the period after the Old Testament to indicate that Judaism, the faith of the Jews, differs significantly from the faith of the Old Testament.

At the time of Jesus' ministry on earth the majority of the Jews were scattered throughout the Mediterranean world and the Middle East, with concentrations in Persia, Mesopotamia, Syria, Egypt, Asia Minor, Greece, and Italy. The Jews, however, still retained interest in the temple and the sacrifices at Jerusalem. For them Jerusalem was the center of the universe. Every Jew tried to make as many pilgrimages there as possible. When the Romans destroyed that temple in AD 70, the primary focus of worship turned to the synagogue.

17

The priests were the guardians of the sacrificial system of worship, but the "scribes" emerged as the teachers of the law. They became the experts who made copies of the Torah, interpreted it, and taught it. They were the professors of theology, whose students, out of respect and admiration, called them "rabbi," literally "my great one" or "master."

The Pharisees developed as a movement of lay people who took seriously the lifestyle that the scribes taught, based on the laws of Moses and their interpretations. Most of the Pharisees were sincere and pious people, and the biblical evidence does not permit us to generalize and call them all hypocrites—though some of the religious leaders with whom Jesus dealt in the Gospels were.

The landscape of Judaism has changed greatly since the writing of the New Testament. The Jewish people who are affiliated with a synagogue or temple today belong to one of the three major branches of Judaism: Orthodox, Conservative, and Reform. As in many Protestant denominations, these divisions are not rigid. The three branches of Judaism have developed historically from the writings of the leaders of the various movements. Much of the teaching of Judaism today still depends on the local rabbi, and what is actually believed by the people varies with the individual. Jewish people even feel free to identify with more than one of these branches or denominations.

None of the three branches of Judaism has a fixed set of doctrines or creeds beyond the *Shema*: "The Lord our God, the Lord is one" (Deuteronomy 6:4; see chapter 3, "What Does Judaism Teach?"). Jews like to say, "If you ask three rabbis, you will get five different opinions." Judaism is monotheistic and oriented mostly to life in this world, with little attention given to life hereafter.

ORTHODOX JUDAISM

The Orthodox Jews refer to themselves as "Torah-true." They are devoted to strict observance of all of the 613 commandments they count in the Torah. The Sabbath must be strictly observed from sundown on Friday to sundown on Saturday. They cannot ride in cars on the Sabbath and can only walk short distances. In biblical times a Sabbath's journey was about three-fourths of a mile, 1,150 meters (Acts 1:12). The Sabbath is observed by complete abstention from work and business. The Orthodox keep "kosher," which means they can eat only the food the Mosaic Law permits (Leviticus 11). They must avoid foods the Law calls "unclean" (such as pork and blood) and must observe such regulations as not drinking milk at the same meal with meat. Furthermore, even for permissible foods, rabbis must supervise the preparation—e.g., the slaughter of animals so that all the blood is drained out of the meat. In Orthodox synagogues the Hebrew language is used, the women are separated from the men, and the head is always covered. Orthodox Jews pray three times a day: morning, late afternoon, and after sunset, with the exact times fixed by the sun.

REFORM JUDAISM

The Orthodox Jews accept the Tanach, the Jewish Bible (which Christians call the Old Testament, except that the order of the books is different), as the inspired, inerrant revelation of God. The Reform (not Reform*ed*) Jew believes in progressive revelation, which takes into account changes brought about by history. Worship occurs in a "temple" rather than a synagogue, sexes can mix, English is generally spoken, and musical instruments are permitted. They do not strictly observe dietary laws. Hope for a personal Messiah is replaced with the hope for a messianic time of peace for humanity. The Reform movement began in Germany as an attempt to modernize the burdensome traditions of Orthodox Judaism, but the center of Reform Judaism today has become the United States.

CONSERVATIVE JUDAISM

Conservative Judaism could be considered a compromise between the strict Orthodox and the liberal Reform. It attempts to keep some of the traditions but still tries to be enlightened by our modern civilization. It keeps some of the dietary laws (with modifications) and uses both Hebrew and English in worship. The Conservative Jew sees Jewish culture as the unifying bond for Jews. The largest number of affiliated Jews belong to this group.

James Limburg, in *Judaism: An Introduction for Christians* (Minneapolis: Augsburg, 1987), suggests that 53 percent of American Jews have no formal membership in a synagogue or temple, but many of them express their "Jewishness" through participation in Jewish organizations. He lists those who are affiliated as Orthodox at 20 percent, Reform 30 percent, and Conservative 50 percent. Other studies and surveys quote similar figures.

OTHER MOVEMENTS WITHIN JUDAISM

There are also other smaller movements and sects within the scope of Judaism. *Hasidic Judaism* is a pietistic movement somewhat akin to the development of the Amish people. It was a reaction against the unemotional Judaism of Eastern Europe. The *Hasidim* (pious ones) sought to express their faith by serving God with joy and even ecstasy.

Zionism is another movement that seeks to colonize Jews in the land of Israel. Zion, the name for the mountain where the temple in Jerusalem was built, came to refer to the temple and then to Jerusalem. In 1896, Theodor Herzl wrote the book *The Jewish State*, which sparked a movement of Jews settling in Palestine. The numbers were small until the State of Israel was founded in 1948 and offered citizenship to any Jew in the world.

Reconstructionism, a radical movement within Judaism, seeks to reconstruct all aspects of Jewish society. It is vehemently rejected by most Jews. Its founder, Mordecai Kaplan,[1] was excommunicated by the Union of Orthodox Rabbis, a rare and unusual event. This movement, while emphasizing the need for a Jewish community, sees that community as a "civilization" rather than a religious community, though the community does have religion as its core. Kaplan even said that the Jewish people are not a people chosen by God—heresy to most Jews.

Many Jewish people of our day espouse no formal religion but take a moralistic approach to the ethical questions of life. They still consider themselves Jews but see their Jewishness not so much as a religion but as a culture, a community of people with a long and rich heritage. These Jews, some of whom are agnostic or atheistic, are sometimes called "cultural Jews" or "secular Jews."

The newest group among the Jewish people are those who identify themselves as *Messianic Jews*. These Jews believe that Jesus of Nazareth is the promised Messiah. Culturally and ethnically they are Jews, but they believe in Jesus Christ as Christians do. Some prefer to use the term *Hebrew Christians, Jewish Christians,* or just plain *believers*. For some the term "Messianic Jew" is confusing, since they see all Jews as being "messianic" in that they all look forward to some type of Messiah or messianic age. Most Jews who do not believe in Jesus claim that the term is deceptive, since it does not identify the Messianic Jew as a follower of Jesus Christ.

The first Lutheran messianic congregation, Beth Messianic Congregation, Queens, New York, was accepted into membership in The Lutheran Church—Missouri Synod in June 1994. The congregation was initiated as a Bible study for Jewish people by Rev. David Born, pastor of the Lutheran Church of Our Saviour, Rego Park, New York. It was first incorporated in January 1984 as Beth Emmanuel fellowship of Queens.

23

The traditional Jewish community today vehemently maintains that when a Jew by birth accepts Jesus as Messiah (that is, when one becomes a Christian), he or she is no longer a Jew. One cannot be a Christian and a Jew at the same time because, they say, these are mutually exclusive categories.

In December 1989 the Israeli Supreme Court ruled that Jews who believe that Jesus is the Messiah cannot be considered Jews under Israel's Law of Return, which guarantees citizenship to every Jew who desires it. The reason, given by Justice Menachem Elon, is that Messianic Jews "do not belong to the Jewish nation. . . . Those who believe in Jesus are in fact Christian." Rabbi A. James Rudin of the American Jewish Committee stated that he hoped this ruling would end the "deceiving charade" of Jews who claim to be Jews but are Christians.[2]

Many Jews who have become Christians, however, strongly object and insist that they are still Jews even though they believe in Jesus. To emphasize their claim, they use terms like *completed Jew, fulfilled Jew,* and call their group a "messianic synagogue" and their spiritual leader "rabbi."

24   Although there are no hard statistics to demonstrate it, more and more Jews who become Christians today want

to continue to be identified with their Jewish heritage. This is true whether they join a messianic congregation or a Gentile congregation. To varying degrees, they want to continue to practice some of their Jewish customs and traditions—the Seder meal of the Passover, circumcision, keeping kosher, wearing yarmulkes and prayer shawls, and using Hebrew in some worship and prayers. In a Gentile congregation this desire can be honored by having group meetings of Jewish believers in addition to the joint worship of the entire congregation. As long as such concerns remain matters of individual practice and not biblical doctrine, we do well to respect the culture and heritage of the Jewish people and allow Jewish believers to express their faith in their own way.

Messianic Judaism has become in recent years similar to a new Protestant denomination. Messianic congregations exist in all major cities of the country that have large Jewish populations. There are several national and world organizations that bring them together in an "association" style. The congregations are independent, though at times loosely connected with some denominations like the Assembly of God or Southern Baptist. Some of them are charismatic. They are Messiah- and Bible-centered and, some have suggested, are somewhat like the congregations in the Early Church.

3 WHAT DOES JUDAISM TEACH?

The three Ecumenical Creeds (the Apostles', the Nicene, and the Athanasian) have for centuries been summary statements of what Christians believe. Individual movements within Christendom have added their own statements of faith and spelled out specific doctrines. In contrast, Judaism has stressed living the faith in this life, putting Jewish beliefs into action, and allowing each individual the freedom to formulate his or her own faith. The Talmud, the major source of postbiblical teachings, is mainly concerned with behavior.

Judaism has no books that systematize Jewish teaching. There are, however, some general, fundamental truths within Judaism. Every morning and evening the faithful Jew is supposed to pray his or her confession, called the *Shema*: "Hear, O Israel: The Lord our God, the Lord is one" (Deuteronomy 6:4). The need for a more detailed summary of Jewish faith was felt strongly when Jewish people settled in other countries of the world where they encountered other religions and entered into debate with them. The thirteen articles, formulated by the Jewish rabbi and scholar Moses Maimonides (AD 1135–1204), make up the closest thing to a creed in Judaism.

I believe . . .

1. That God alone is Creator.
2. That He is absolutely One.
3. That He has no body or bodily shape.
4. That He is the first and the last.
5. That only to Him may we pray and to no other.
6. That the words of the prophets are true.
7. That the prophecy of Moses is true, and that he is the father of all prophets.
8. That the Torah was given by Moses.
9. That this Torah is not subject to change, and that there will never be another Torah from the Creator.
10. That the Creator knows all the thoughts and deeds of man.
11. That He rewards and punishes according to the deed.
12. That the Messiah will come; though He tarry, I will expect Him daily.
13. That the dead will be resurrected.

It is, however, not necessary for an individual Jew to sub-scribe to every detail of these statements. They were considered a valid confession by Maimonides, and they can be the basis for formulating what a Jewish person *chooses* to believe today. Christians, of course, often want to know what Jews believe about specific items. But that cannot be answered any more specifically than it can among the two thousand different Christian denom-inations. With that caution in mind, here is an attempt to state in a general way what many Jews believe about cer-tain articles of faith.

THE BIBLE

Judaism has often been called a religion of the book. Every synagogue keeps one scroll of the Torah, the first five books of Moses (Genesis, Exodus, Leviticus, Numbers, Deuteronomy), enshrined in a special "ark" or cabinet in the front of the synagogue. Together, the Torah scroll and a congregation make a synagogue, that is, a place set apart for Jewish study and worship.

The Torah, sometimes translated "law," together with the other thirty-four books that comprise the Old Testament used by Protestant Christians, make up the Jewish Bible. The other thirty-four books are divided into two cate-gories: "prophets" and "writings." Jews call their Bible the Tanach (*t*, *n*, and *ch* are the first letters of the Hebrew words for Torah, prophets, and writings). Some Jews resent it when Christians call the Tanach the "Old Testament" since they do not believe that there is a "New Testament," or "New Covenant." To avoid offense some Gentiles have substituted the terms "Hebrew Scriptures" and "Greek Scriptures."

Orthodox Jews believe that the Tanach is the inspired, inerrant Word revealed by God. Most Jews also consider the "oral Torah"—given to Moses and passed down orally by the rabbis until it was recorded in the Talmud—to be God's Word. Other branches of Judaism take a more liberal view, seeing revelation as progressive and the Scriptures as merely human writings.

The Talmud is a 2,700-page record of oral tradition passed down by ancient rabbis in Hebrew and Aramaic. It consists of stories, proverbs, moral reasonings, and observations on all manner of human endeavor. The English translation is not complete. Some Jews read a "daf" (both sides of one page) a day, and thus they can read the entire Talmud in seven and a half years (*St. Louis Post Dispatch*, April 29, 1990). While the Talmud is not considered inspired and inerrant, it still informs a important part of Judaic beliefs.

29

THE MESSIAH

Judaism has always been strongly messianic. The prophets promised a "greater prophet" than Moses, a king who would restore the throne of David, a Suffering Servant who would redeem His people. Every Jewish mother at the time of Jesus hoped that her son would be the Messiah. However, many Jews in Jesus' day did not welcome Jesus as the Messiah because they conceived of the Messiah as a political king who would free them from Gentile rule and establish once again the glory of Israel. They generally ignored prophecies such as Isaiah 53 and Psalm 22, which said that the Messiah would suffer and die for the sins of the people.

But Jesus came, and the Jews had to deal with Him. After Pentecost, the Church grew as the apostles preached that the crucified and risen Jesus was truly the Messiah who fulfilled all of the prophecies. The officials had to take a stand. There were strong differences of opinion. The Sanhedrin issued the order "not to speak or teach at all in the name of Jesus" (Acts 4:18). The conflict that then unfolded between the Church and the synagogue helped to shape the development of Judaism. One thing remained a strong element in Judaism: it was anti-Jesus. Judaism clearly taught that Jesus of Nazareth was *not* the Messiah.

Judaism, however, did remain messianic in the sense that Jewish people continued to look forward to the coming of the Messiah. The Reform branch, however, no longer expects a personal Messiah but looks forward to the coming of a messianic age of peace and good will. This was expressed by a Jewish lawyer at a Messianic Forum luncheon in St. Louis: "When I see the lamb and the lion lie down together, as Isaiah promised, I will believe the Messiah has come."

ONE GOD

Judaism has always maintained a strict and unyielding monotheism. Their common confession of the *Shema* sums it up for the Jews. "The Lord our God, the Lord is one" (Deuteronomy 6:4). Jewish theology explains what *one God* means in these four ways:

1. God is one, not many. Judaism separates itself from any type of polytheism.

2. God is one, not two. Judaism rejects any form of dualism, as evidenced in traditional Zoroastrianism.

3. God is one, not three. Judaism rejects the Christian teaching of the Trinity, that God is one essence but three persons. (Jews mistakenly insist Christians teach that there are three Gods: Father, Son and Holy Spirit.)

4. God is one, not none. Judaism declares its opposition to atheism. (Today there are some Jews, however, who are atheists, but they still consider themselves Jews.)

PEOPLE—SIN—SALVATION

People are made in the image of God, Judaism teaches. Thus they are inherently good and capable of doing God's will. Besides their good nature, people also have a "yetzer hara," an evil inclination that may lead them astray. But this evil inclination does not compare to the Christian teaching of the sinful human nature, or original sin. Since people are inherently good according to Judaism, if they sin, they are capable of achieving their own forgiveness. This forgiveness, while it comes from God, is earned through repentance, prayer, and doing good deeds. The sinner must take the initiative and deserve it.

The Jewish holidays (for example, *Yom Kippur*, the Day of Atonement) provide formal opportunities for Jewish people to achieve this forgiveness. In the Old Testament, Yom Kippur was the day when the high priest made sacrificial atonement (covering) for his own sins and the sins of the people. Today, Jews observe the Day of Atonement with Ten Days of Awe preceding it, days for personal reflection, repentance, prayer, and forgiving others—all in order to receive forgiveness for themselves.

With this view of humanity and sin, most Jewish people see no need for a savior from sin who will mediate between people and God. Rabbi Hillel Silver, in the book *Where Judaism Differed*, writes, "The key Protestant doctrine of Justification by Faith alone, and not through good works, finds no place in Judaism."[1] John Wilch, in the Lenten Bible Study "Jesus' Passion—the Jewish People and We Christians," lists in a structured way these summary statements of the Jewish view of salvation:

Judaism in the first century was dominated by three things:

1. the *temple* at Jerusalem, with all its ritual sacrifices;

2. the *Sabbath day*, around which an overwhelming burden of prohibitions had gathered; and

3. the *law* of God, originally given to Moses, written down in the Tanach, and interpreted by the Talmud and the clergy of the day.

To please God one had to walk this threefold route. (Michael Green, *Who Is This Jesus*).

1. Everyone has access to God directly, depending upon his own initiative to turn to God.

2. Everyone has a free will and can overcome evil inclinations by his will and with God's help.

33

3. All Jews, because of their election by God as His people, are already essentially saved.

4. This salvation can be forfeited by severe crimes and the refusal to repent.

5. But if one sincerely repents, tries to make up for wrongs to other people, and strives to do good works for one's fellow man, one will atone for all misdeeds and be assured of God's grace and eternal life.

6. Essential for this view is that the Jew believe in the God of Israel, study the Torah of Moses (as well as its commentaries in the other Scriptures, in the Talmud, and in writings by more recent scholars), and endeavor to live according to God's will. (Task Force on Witnessing to Jewish People, The Lutheran Church—Missouri Synod, 1983)

IMMORTALITY

Most Jewish people live for today, says Steve Cohen, a Jewish believer in Jesus, though he admits that the more religious ones do focus on the world to come. The Reform Jews and nonreligious Jews have little concern for a life after death. Instead they focus their attention on making this earth a better place to live both for themselves and those who come after them. The Jewish faith spans a broad range of beliefs about immortality. Some Jews even deny an afterlife. The most religious, or Orthodox, Jews do hope for a life "with the fathers" in the future, though that life is not very well defined.

Just as there was a difference of opinion among the Pharisees and the Sadducees over the resurrection of the dead (Matthew 22:23–33), so there are many differences of opinion among Jews today about heaven and hell. Jews think of the terms *heaven* and *hell* as primarily Christian concerns. Jewish writings do refer to "the Bosom of Herahaur" and "the Pit of Sheol" as places of the dead or of punishment, but the teachings are very vague. Some very religious Jews think of "Gar Edeun," paradise, as the reward for a righteous life of keeping the commandments. In any case, whatever hope a Jew has for a life after death, it is completely dependent upon good deeds done here on earth.

PRAYER

The devout Jew spends his life in praising God as the Creator and Lord of both the whole universe and each individual life. Therefore, the events of the day are to be accompanied by prayers of praise, blessing, petition, and repentance. Jews awaken the day with the morning prayer and conclude the day with the evening prayer. Mealtimes are also important times of prayer. Jewish prayer is strong on praise—as in the traditional *berakhah,* or word of blessing: *Baruch atah, Adonai Eloheinu, melech ha'olam* (Praised are You, Lord our God, King of the universe).

Jewish worship is prayer centered, both in the home as well as in the synagogue. Over the years, prayers in Hebrew have been added to the psalms and printed together with other worship texts in the Jewish prayer book, the *siddur*.

Jewish prayer is connected with certain rituals such as washing the hands and wearing a prayer shawl (*tallith*) to cover the head as a sign of humility. Phylacteries (*tefillin*) are worn during morning prayer on weekdays, though not on the Sabbath or holidays. These are small leather cubes tied on the forehead and left arm with leather straps. The cubes contain passages of Scripture, and thus carry out the command "to bind them [God's commandments] as a sign on your hand, and they shall be as frontlets between your eyes" (Deuteronomy 6:8).

When a Jew prays, the hands are not folded, but the arms are extended and raised to God with open palms facing up. Some Jews also move the upper part of the body back and forth while praying. Those who visit the Wailing Wall in Jerusalem witness this activity. It is a mark of pious prayer. Some authorities trace this swaying of the body while praying or reading the Torah to the concept that the Jew is attached to the Torah as a flame is attached to a candle.[2]

The practice of prayer is much the same in all branches of Judaism, though the Reform allows more room for prayer in English, for free prayer, and for women's participation.

SOME COMMON PRACTICES

The Mezuzah (Doorpost)

Many Jewish people put Scripture passages in a small container and fix it on the doorframe of their homes to carry out the directions of Deuteronomy 6:6–9 to meditate on the commandments as you go out and come in through the door. These little containers are often made into beautiful ornaments.

The Jewish calendar is based on the cycle of the moon rather than the sun. The lunar year has 354 days. A leap month is added in the third, sixth, eighth, eleventh, fourteenth, seventeenth and nineteenth years of a nineteen-year cycle. Jews count years from the creation of the world, so that 2010 is 5770–71 (their new year begins in September or October). Instead of BC (before Christ) and AD (*anno Domini*, in the year of the Lord), they use BCE (before the common era) and CE (common era).

37

Some Jews will kiss their fingers and touch the mezuzah as they pass through the door, almost like a good luck charm.

The Star of David

The Star of David, known as the Magen David, is often used as a symbol of the Jewish people. Many Jews wear it in some form of jewelry or use it as a decorative identification. When the new nation of Israel was born in 1948, it became the dominant symbol on the national flag. The Star of David is a six-pointed star, one triangle inverted on top of another. The traditional star of Bethlehem, or Christmas star, has five points. There is much speculation about the symbolism and the origin of the Star of David, but little definite information is known.

The Menorah

The menorah, a seven-branched candelabrum patterned after the one used in the tabernacle/temple, is used to symbolize the belief that the Jewish people are the lights to the Gentiles. A different type of menorah is used during the Jewish celebration of Hanukkah. The Hanukkah menorah has eight branches, plus the *shammes*, the helper or servant candle, which is used to light the others. One candle is lit on each of the eight days of Hanukkah as a reminder of the single day's supply of sacred oil that Jews believe lasted for eight days while the temple was cleansed and new sacred oil provided.

The menorah has become perhaps the most popular identification of the Jewish people in America, almost a symbol of the Jewish people rather than the Jewish faith. Where Christians use a crèche (manger scene), Jews use a menorah. For example, the Supreme Court ruled in July 1989 that Allegheny County in Pennsylvania could not display a crèche, a symbol of Christianity, on the city-county building. However, the city of Pittsburgh was allowed to keep its menorah, a symbol of Judaism, since it was set beside a "secular" symbol, a Christmas tree. (Rather than use a secular symbol like Santa Claus instead of the crèche, the local governments removed both the crèche and menorah.)

Circumcision

In obedience to the command to circumcise male infants on the eighth day as a sign of God's everlasting covenant (Genesis 17:9–14; Leviticus 12:3), most Jewish people continue to circumcise their baby boys. In the Bible, days were counted inclusively, so the eighth day is exactly one week from the birth. The circumcision, or *briss*, is performed by a rabbi or a person authorized to do it: a

39

mohel. With special ceremonies and prayers the rabbi or mohel cuts the foreskin from the end of the penis with a sharp knife. God said that when this is done, the boy becomes a child of the covenant. In the Bible, there is no similar ceremony for girls. Today baby girls are named, usually in the synagogue, on the first Sabbath after their birth. Christians believe that the ceremonial laws of the Mosaic covenant, including the command to circumcise, are not mandatory in the new covenant established by Jesus. For Christians, Baptism replaces circumcision as the way to enter the kingdom of God.

Bar-Mitzvah/Bat-Mitzvah

At the age of thirteen, after proper instruction, a Jewish boy goes through a bar mitzvah, similar to a Christian confirmation. For girls there is a bat-mitzvah at age twelve. *Bar* means "son," and *bat* means "daughter." *Mitzvah* means "commandment." When a child thus becomes a son or daughter of the commandment, he or she is recognized as an adult for religious purposes and has full standing in the religious community.

4 RESPONDING WITH APPRECIATION

Today the Christian Church is largely Gentile, but it was not always so. The Early Christian Church in New Testament times was Jewish. The leaders were Jewish and the members were Jewish. The believers in the Old Testament, God's chosen people, were called the Israelites rather than the Church. They were the ones through whom God's plan of salvation was carried out. The Messiah, Jesus, was ethnically a Jew.

We Gentiles owe a great debt of gratitude to the Jewish people. We are the "wild olive shoot[s]" that were grafted in (Romans 11:17), while the Jews, the original branches, were broken off because of their unbelief. Paul expressed appreciation and respect for the Jewish people and listed specific reasons: "They are Israelites, and to them belong the adoption, the glory, the covenants, the giving of the law, the worship, and the promises. To them belong the patriarchs, and from their race, according to the flesh, is the Christ who is God over all, blessed forever. Amen" (Romans 9:4–5).

WITH APPRECIATION FOR JESUS

God honored the Jewish people by sending the Messiah through their race. Martin Luther expressed his appreciation to the Jews by writing a book in 1523 entitled *That Jesus Christ Was Born a Jew* in which he says,

> When we are inclined to boast of our position we should remember that we are but Gentiles, while the Jews are of the lineage of Christ. We are aliens and in-laws; they are blood relatives, cousins, and brothers of our Lord. Therefore, if one is to boast of flesh and blood, the Jews are actually nearer to Christ than we are.[1]

The father of the Jews, Abraham, is also our spiritual father; it is not based on circumcision any longer. Paul says, "The purpose was to make [Abraham] the father of all who believe without being circumcised, so that righteousness would be counted to them as well" (Romans 4:11). That does not give us the right to call ourselves Jews, as some fundamentalist Christians have done, for Abraham is our *spiritual* father, the father of all who claim salvation in his seed, the Jew Jesus Christ.

Gentile Christians, grafted into the olive tree trunk, whose roots are Christ, with Abraham as their father, are now part of a new chosen race. Peter applies terms used for God's Old Testament people to the New Testament Christians who are both Jew and Gentile. "You are a chosen people, a royal priesthood, a holy nation, a people for [God's] own possession" (1 Peter 2:9).

In Galatians 6:16, Paul uses another term for New Testament believers. Together, Jew and Gentile are the "Israel of God." Some Christians speak of the "new Israel," comprised of all believers in Christ. This is not a biblical term and offends some Jewish believers. To them it implies that the "old Israel" has been eliminated and replaced with the "new Israel." This suggests that the original Israel, the descendants of Abraham in the flesh, no longer exists. It is better to use the biblical term "Israel of God" (or even "the Israel of the New Testament") when describing the Christian Church made up of Jews and Gentiles.

Jewish believers in Jesus point out that God has not rejected the Jewish people. They quote St. Paul who says, "God has not rejected His people. . . . For the gifts and calling of God are irrevocable" (Romans 11:2, 29). God is still faithful to His promises and has preserved the Jewish people despite the hate, the persecutions, and the attempts by the Gentiles to annihilate them. They continue to exist as a constant reminder of God's past covenant with them. In order not to offend Jewish people and at the same time be more biblical in our language, it would be better not to use the term *new Israel*.

It should be noted, however, that being of the chosen race does not bring personal salvation. Salvation is a matter of faith, and there have always been Jews of the chosen race who were not saved. Paul says, "For not all who are descended from Israel belong to Israel" (Romans 9:6).

WITH APPRECIATION FOR CHURCH DESIGN

Many elements of our worship life were shaped by our roots in Judaism. The pastor wears robes as he conducts the service, following the example of the priests in the tabernacle/temple. Traditional church buildings face the east, pointing toward Jerusalem, where the synagogues in Babylon faced.

The nave and chancel arrangement, divided by the communion rail, imitate the tabernacle and the temple division of the Holy Place and the Most Holy Place. The communion rail represents the ancient dividing curtain.

In most Christian church buildings, however, the communion rail opens directly in front of the altar. This opening does not just allow worship leaders easy access to the altar, but symbolizes open access to God for all believers. Through Jesus, the Great High Priest who made the final and complete sacrifice, we can come directly into the presence of God.

The altar reminds us of the altar on which offerings were brought to God and sacrifices made to Him. It reminds us of the entire Mosaic covenant with all of its laws and prescribed rituals that were fulfilled by Jesus, the Lamb of God. The altar also reminds us of the Passover table where the meal was shared and at which Jesus instituted the Lord's Supper. The sanctuary lamp found in many churches has its counterpart in the "eternal light," or *ner tamid*, of the ancient tabernacle and modern synagogues.

WITH APPRECIATION FOR WORSHIP PATTERNS

Today's liturgical style of Christian worship was patterned after the style of worship in the synagogue. Jewish worship has always followed a fixed calendar of religious holidays, which were reminders of God's involvement with His people. The observant Jew today delights in the round of holidays just as liturgically sensitive Christians appreciate the drama and beauty of the Christian Church Year, which reminds them of Christ's work in atoning for their sins.

The most important Jewish holidays are listed below in their chronological order, with the approximate time of the year. Since the Jewish calendar is lunar, the specific dates vary each year.

1. New Year: Rosh Hashanah, September–October
2. Day of Atonement: Yom Kippur, September–October
3. Tabernacles or Booths: Sukkoth, September–October
4. Festival of Lights: Hanukkah, November–December
5. Day of Lots: Purim, February–March
6. Passover: Pesah, March–April
7. Pentecost: Shavuoth, May–June

Christians not only copied the concept of a yearly religious calendar from the Jews, but also absorbed the Jewish concept of appointed readings for each week's worship. The pattern in the synagogue is to read an assigned lesson from the Torah and then one from the prophetic writings. The readings are arranged so that the entire Torah will be read in a year. The Christian Church kept the concept but developed its own set of readings to include portions from the Old Testament, an Epistle, and a Gospel.

WITH APPRECIATION FOR THE PASSOVER

46   God commanded the Passover observance as a way for Israel to remember how, in the tenth plague, the angel

of death passed over the homes of the Hebrews while slaying the firstborn throughout Egypt. By repeating the Passover meal, often called the Seder, they were to "experience" each year the deliverance of their ancestors from slavery to the freedom of the Promised Land.

While this holiday is distinctively Jewish, more and more Christian groups today observe the Seder, using many of the traditional customs of the Jewish people. Christians differ, however, in that they observe the Seder to remind themselves of the institution of the Lord's Supper and the freedom they have in Christ from slavery to sin, as well as to celebrate the exodus deliverance of their spiritual forefathers.

It was during the Passover meal with His disciples that Jesus took the unleavened bread, the matzah, and gave it to His disciples and said, "This is My body." He took the wine of the Passover meal, gave it to His disciples, and said, "This is My blood of the covenant, which is poured out for many for the forgiveness of sins" (Matthew 26:26, 28). Jesus fulfilled all the symbolism of the exodus and the Passover by His sacrifice on the altar of Calvary. As Paul wrote, "Christ, our Passover lamb, has been sacrificed" (1 Corinthians 5:7).

5 RESPONDING TO ANTI-SEMITISM

In 1492 King Ferdinand and Queen Isabella signed the Edict of Expulsion, which gave Spanish Jews, called Sephardic (Hebrew for Spain; but see Obadiah 20) Jews, four months to convert to Catholicism or to be expelled. About half (200,000) scattered to other countries, while others converted, though many of them were suspect. In 1992, Spain formally revoked the edict on its five-hundredth anniversary and gave the Jewish faith equal status with Catholicism.

"His blood be on us and on our children!" Thus "all the people" answered when Pilate washed his hands and said, "I am innocent of this man's blood" (Matthew 27:24–25). Did these words bring a curse on all Jewish people for all time? Some early Christians interpreted it this way. These words, together with the role of the Jewish leaders in plotting for and demanding Jesus' death, became the source of anti-Semitic attitudes. Today's anti-Semitism, however, comes from a general animosity toward Jewish people and not from this scriptural pretext. Yet, it still happens that a Jewish child is ridiculed by playmates and called "Christ-killer."

How do we deal with the concept of "Christ-killer"? Some points to remember and study:

- Only a small group of religious leaders turned over Jesus to be crucified.

- God did not curse all Jews in all centuries because of those Jews who cried, "Crucify Him."

- In the believers' prayer of Acts 4:27, the blame for the crucifixion is laid at the feet of Herod, Pontius Pilate, the Gentiles, and the people of Israel.

- Jesus prayed, "Father, forgive them, for they know not what they do" (Luke 23:34).

- A follower of Jesus loves even his or her enemies.

- Jesus willingly laid down His life to atone for the sins of the whole world, Jews and Gentiles alike (1 John 2:2, Galatians 3:26–29). His life was not taken—it was given.

It is regrettable that by the fourth century, the highly respected and influential church leader John Chrysostom called the Jews the "most miserable" of all people— "lustful, rapacious, greedy, perfidious bandits." Because of their "odious assassination of Christ," he said, there is "no expiation possible, no indulgence, no pardon."

He concluded that since God hates the Jews and cursed them, it is the duty of Christians to hate them too.

Other church leaders followed a similar pattern, so that anti-Semitism reached a disastrous climax during the Crusades. In the Crusades of AD 1096, 1144, and 1189, Christians in Europe were stirred up first to free the Holy Land from the Muslims, the "enemies of God." Feeding on its own frenzy, the extremism continued: "It is ridiculous to go to a distant land to kill God's enemies, the Muslims, while the Jews, who are also God's enemies and opposed to Christianity, are close at hand." Eventually the cry rang throughout Europe, "Kill a Jew and save your soul!" Approximately ten thousand Jews lost their lives in central Europe just because they were Jews. Jews in the Holy Land were also murdered. In one incident, a crusading army captured Jerusalem from Muslims and then drove all the Jewish inhabitants of the city into the synagogue and set it on fire, singing a Christian hymn while the flames destroyed the Jews.

Anti-Semitism broke out again during the Inquisition, which began in Spain in the fifteenth century. It sought to identify insincere Jewish converts (called "Marranos," "pigs") and discipline them. These "insincere converts" were Jews who outwardly had "converted" due to threats and public pressure, but who continued secretly to practice Judaism. Thousands of Jews were tortured and burned alive at public executions.

Martin Luther was also caught up in the anti-Semitism of the sixteenth century. During his earlier ministry he was very concerned about the conversion of the Jews and wrote five books about them. By 1543, Luther was disappointed over the Jews' failure to convert and angered at their blasphemy of Christ. Caught up in a "literary temper tantrum," he wrote his infamous book *On the Jews and Their Lies*. He called them a "condemned and rejected people" and listed a seven-point program on how to deal with them:

1. Set fire to their synagogues and schools and cover with dirt whatever will not burn.
2. Raze and destroy their homes.
3. Take away their prayer books and Talmudic writings. In them is idolatry, lies, cursing, and blasphemy.
4. Forbid the rabbis to teach on pain of loss of life and limb.
5. Abolish safe conduct on the highways for Jews.
6. Take all cash, silver, and gold from them and hold it for safekeeping.
7. Put into the hands of the young, strong Jews …an ax, a hoe, a spade, a spindle and let them earn their bread by the sweat of their brow.[1]

Ever since Luther wrote those words, Lutherans have been offended and scandalized by them. It is good to remember that in Luther's final sermon, preached three days before his death in 1546, he said:

> We want to act in a Christian way toward them and offer them first of all the Christian faith, that they might accept the Messiah, who after all, is their kinsman and born of their flesh and blood and is of the real seed of Abraham of which they boast. . . . We want to treat them with Christian love and pray for them, so that they might be converted and would receive the Lord.

The Lutheran Church—Missouri Synod dealt with Luther's anti-Semitic writings in its 1983 convention and passed a resolution (3–09), which said in its third "Resolved":

> While . . . we are deeply indebted to Luther for his rediscovery and enunciation of the Gospel, . . . we deplore and disassociate ourselves from Luther's negative statements about the Jewish people, and . . . we deplore the use today of such sentiments by Luther to incite anti-Christian and/or anti-Lutheran sentiment.[2]

52   In 1994, the Church Council of the Evangelical Lutheran Church in America (ELCA) passed a similar resolution in

which they rejected "this violent invective." They went on to express "our deep and abiding sorrow over its tragic effect on subsequent generations."

Murderous persecution again exploded against the Jews in this century in the form of the Holocaust, which destroyed one-third of the Jewish world population. Adolph Hitler and his followers tried desperately to eliminate the Jewish race. The overt action began on November 20, 1938, on *Krystallnacht*, the night of terror in which over one hundred Jews died, seventy-five hundred Jewish shops were looted, and six hundred synagogues were burned. By January 1, all Jewish businesses in Germany were liquidated. Forced labor followed, then concentration camps and extermination. By the end of the war, six million Jews had been killed.

Anti-Semitism is a prejudice that grows out of human sinful nature. By His grace, God does forgive Christians for their anti-Semitic feelings and actions. Subsequently, Christians can learn to love Jews as they love all people—and in that spirit share with them the Good News that Jesus offers forgiveness, new life, and eternal life to everyone who will believe in Him.

6 RESPONDING AS A CONGREGATION

Upon graduating from seminary, I served as pastor in several congregations in southern Illinois for fourteen years. I was not personally acquainted with any Jewish people during those years. I surely knew some business or professional men who were Jewish, but I was not aware of their ancestry at that time. The story was the same when I served nine years on a college campus in Seward, Nebraska. During those twenty-four years I had no concern about telling Jewish people the Gospel.

The first time I sensed a need to witness to Jewish people occurred at an evangelism weekend at a congregation in Buffalo, New York. I was helping the pastor arrange for a door-to-door survey on Saturday afternoon when he pointed to one area on the map near the church and said, "We can't go into that area. Those people are Jewish." "Why?" I asked. "Isn't the Gospel for Jewish people too? Are we afraid of them? Do we believe they are rejected by God? Do we think it wouldn't do any good?"

Those are the excuses I have repeatedly heard since then for what might be called the "Christian passover"—passing over the Jewish people as we spread the Gospel of Jesus Christ. Paul said that the Gospel "is the power of God for salvation . . . to the Jew first and also to the Greek" (Romans 1:16). Today Jewish people are more open about their Jewishness and proud of it. The daily news makes us conscious of Jewish organizations, a Jewish state, the Jewish vote, and anti Semitic acts against the Jews. Jews live in most large cities of the country, and most congregations are aware of them in their communities.

How do we respond? Our commission from the Lord is to "make disciples of all nations" (Matthew 28:18–20), to be His witnesses "to the ends of the earth" (Acts 1:8). The response of a congregation toward Jewish people ought to be this: "How can we share with them the Good News that Jesus is the Messiah?" This chapter discusses how a congregation can cultivate and implement that response.

NURTURE A SPIRIT OF WITNESS

When a Jewish believer, Steve Cohen, first came to know Jesus as the Messiah through the influence and prayers of a Lutheran friend, he began to attend a Lutheran church in his hometown, Seattle. In Bible class, when there was a chance to ask questions, he inquired as to how Lutherans tell others about their faith in Jesus. All he knew was that his friend, Alan, had prayed for him for two years and shared the Bible with him. Steve was not prepared for the answer of a lady in the class: "We Lutherans don't do that sort of thing."

In many congregations the real need is not just to nurture a concern to witness to Jewish people, but rather a concern to witness to *all* people. If the congregation will not intentionally reach out to Gentiles, it will be less likely to reach out Jewish people. An evangelistic attitude must permeate all of the teaching and preaching of a congregation. That attitude must view the mission of the Church as not only giving money to send missionaries or caring for the physical needs of others, but of making disciples of everyone in the community. Every Christian is an ambassador for Christ, entrusted with the "message of reconciliation" that God wants us to share with our friends, neighbors, relatives, and everyone in our community (2 Corinthians 5:17–21).

SENSITIZE TO THE NEED TO WITNESS TO JEWISH PEOPLE

Christians in the United States are caught up in pluralistic thinking that puts a high priority on toleration and acceptance. Americans want to think that all religions are equally valid. Sincerity is the only criterion for belief. Accompanying this attitude is individualism. Gallup documented an expression of this individualism in *The Unchurched American 1988*. In that survey, 80 percent of those polled said that one should arrive at his or her own beliefs without the help of a church or synagogue.

Pluralistic thinking strongly resists the claim that Jesus is the only way of salvation (John 14:6; Acts 4:12) and that all who do not believe in Him will be damned (Mark 16:16; John 8:24). To insist on this scriptural teaching one must conclude that the Jewish person's faith, in whatever type of Judaism is espoused, is inadequate because Jesus, the Messiah, is not the object of faith. Jewish people generally respond to this truth, as do some Gentiles, by calling it intolerant, narrow-minded bigotry, even anti-Semitic.

Many Christians want to avoid calling the Jewish faith inadequate, and yet they want to be faithful to the biblical teaching that salvation only comes through Jesus. This presents a dilemma. It cannot be both ways. Some Christians have dealt with this problem by adopting the "two covenant" theory. This approach maintains that there is no need to witness to Jewish people because they can be saved if they believe in their Tanach (the

Christian's Old Testament) and are faithful to it. When the American Lutheran Church (ALC) issued a document dealing with the Jewish people in 1974, it used language like this (emphasis added):

> *Some Lutherans* find in Scripture clear directions to bear missionary witness in which conversion is hoped for.

> *Others hold* that when Scripture speaks about the relation between Jews and Christians, its central theme is that God's promises to Israel have not been abrogated.

The document explained that one approach tries to bring Jews into the Body of Christ. The other approach tends to see the Church and the Jewish people as together forming one people of God, separated from one another for the time being, yet with the promise that they will ultimately be one. This view directly contradicts Ephesians 2:11–18, which states that believing Jews and Gentiles are united in Christ *now*.

On the basis of Scripture, The Lutheran Church—Missouri Synod has repeatedly stated an opposing view through convention resolutions—as it did in 1979 when it adopted a "Statement of Jewish Lutheran Concerns" (Resolution

1-30, St. Louis). In this resolution the Missouri Synod states its position as follows:

1. We Desire to Be *Sensitive.*
2. We Plead for *Understanding.*
3. We State Our *Commitment.*

The commitment statement in this resolution includes these words:

> The words of Jesus remain true for us today: "I am the Way and the Truth and the Life; no one comes to the Father but by Me" (John 14:6); as do the words of Peter: "There is salvation in no one else, for there is no other name [than the name of Jesus] under heaven given among men by which we must be saved" (Acts 4:12).
>
> . . . We are obligated to share the Gospel of Jesus as Lord and Savior with all people, Jew and Gentile alike (Matthew 28:18–20; Luke 24:46–49), and we seek to follow the example of our Lord and the early apostles with the zeal expressed by St. Paul when he said, "My heart's desire and prayer to God for them [Jews] is that they may be saved" (Romans 10:1).[1]

BE INTENTIONAL

If we are serious in our concern for witnessing to Jewish people, we need to develop ways in which to do it and consciously strive to accomplish it. We cannot assume that it will happen spontaneously. The unique nature of Jewish-Christian relationships and the attitudes that have been shaped through the history of those relationships work against it.

A beginning list of specific things a congregation can do to witness intentionally to Jewish people and to help its members witness to them in their daily contacts provides a starting point. Here is such a list:

> The Jewish community protested a workshop in Milwaukee to help Christians understand Jewish people and share their faith with their Jewish neighbors in a loving way. The president of the Milwaukee Jewish Council issued a public statement objecting, saying that the Jewish community is "under siege." Any effort at proselytizing, he said, is against American freedom of religion and cannot be allowed.

1. Assign the responsibility. Everyone's task often becomes no one's. It is best to assign to one board or committee the focus on relationships with and witness to the Jewish people in the community. This group can

60

monitor what is happening, initiate activities, and help shape attitudes. Many of the following suggestions can be carried out by this board or committee.

2. Discover the Jews in the community. How many Jewish people live in the area that the congregation considers its area of outreach? Are there synagogues or temples in the area? Reform, Conservative, Orthodox? How religious are the people in the community? What is the background of the Jews in the community: recent immigrants, Americans for a hundred years?

3. Assess the needs of the congregation. What is needed to build positive attitudes toward outreach in the congregation? If the congregation has had little contact with Jewish people, one need might be awareness. This could include visits to synagogues and temples, attending Jewish community events, or planning Christian-Jewish events such as "An Evening of Understanding." At such a gathering Jewish and Christian speakers each might share (not debate) some customs and beliefs of their faith.

4. Organize for witness. When the committee has an understanding of the Jewish people in the community and general knowledge of the attitudes of congregation members, it is time to plan for outreach. Begin with specific goals, and then develop strategies necessary to carry them out. Some things to include are the following:

- Make additional contacts with Jewish people as mentioned above.

- Review the educational program of the church, both that of children and adults. Are opportunities provided to learn about modern day Jews, to understand their holidays, and to avoid negative teachings that result in anti-Semitic attitudes?

- Provide classes or workshops for members, and help them learn to witness to Jewish people (see chapter 7, "Responding as an Individual").

- Establish a file of Jewish people who are open to witness, and develop a mailing and calling program. This may even be part of the regular evangelism program of the congregation.

5. Develop a library for Jewish-Christian relations. The average church member has little or no access to material that could help in understanding Jewish people—their history, beliefs, and current situation. A special section of the congregational library could be devoted to such topics as Jewish holidays, the Holocaust, the state of Israel, modern Jewish life and practice, anti-Semitism, how to witness to Jewish people, and fulfillment of prophecy.

62

6. Deal with anti-Semitism. Most of us hold latent anti-Semitic attitudes. Jokes and old clichés about Jews having all the money and controlling business and the media subconsciously shape our attitude toward Jews. The issues surrounding the Israeli-Palestinian strife also needs to be discussed and addressed. Deal with latent or overt anti-Semitism if it is prevalent in your congregation. Confront prejudice and anti-Semitism in the entire preaching and teaching program of the congregation.

7. Support Jewish missionary agencies.

Independent missionary agencies that specialize in a specific mission (such as witnessing to Jewish people) offer resources and expertise to support the congregation's efforts. They can also reach Jewish people beyond the boundaries of a given parish. (See the list of such agencies in "Resources: Agencies," at the end of this book.)

Interdenominational agencies such as Jews for Jesus often have traveling teams that present musical and educational programs in local congregations. One of the most helpful is a presentation of "Christ in the Passover," which explains the connection and symbolism of the Passover and the Lord's Supper. Individual members who contribute to these agencies usually do not use funds that would otherwise support their local parish. They receive from these agencies newsletters and materials relating to Jewish evangelism. By encouraging support of these agencies, we strengthen our attitudes toward Jewish people and our need to witness to them.

8. Encourage personal ministry. Some Jewish missionary agencies need volunteers to help in their administrative functions, as well as in special outreach projects. They usually also offer training for this ministry. The Lutheran Church—Missouri Synod, in cooperation with The Apple of His Eye (AOHE) Mission Society, sponsors summer "street witnessing" in various major cities across the United States. These events not only provide opportunities for witnessing, but they strengthen the volunteer and motivate him or her to return to his or her home congregation to help establish an ongoing witness to Jewish people.

7 RESPONDING TO YOUR JEWISH NEIGHBOR

Much of what is said in chapter 6 about "Responding as a Congregation" also applies to responding as an individual. But here are some specific suggestions for the individual who seeks to actively witness to Jewish people.

1. Be a friend. Love is the basic characteristic of the disciple of Jesus Christ (John 13:34–35). Our love is like God's love: unconditional. It does not depend on how our Jewish neighbor treats us, whether the neighbor accepts our witness or mocks it. Love is more than bait to get a hearing for the Gospel. It includes genuine concern, respect, and care for the person.

2. Discuss life issues. Discussing life issues will give you some insight on how your friends perceive and think. Ask them what their Jewish beliefs mean to them. Avoid giving any impression that you want to be a friend merely to convert them.

3. Be sensitive. In a loving relationship, the Christian seeks to be sensitive to the feelings of the Jewish person and tactfully to avoid what offends his or her sensitivities. Some language suggestions are given below to replace words and expressions that offend some Jewish people, although not all of them. Using terms that do not offend creates a better climate for conversation and facilitates communication.

Instead of . . .	say . . .
Christ	Messiah
Jew	Jewish person
convert	Jewish believer
Bible	Scriptures
Old Testament	the Tanach, or Hebrew Bible
New Testament	Greek Bible, or Christian New Testament
church	congregation

In addition, some Jewish people prefer to call Jesus by His Hebrew name, Yeshua (pronounced Yes-SHOO-ah).

Furthermore, effectiveness in witnessing requires that you know whether the Jewish person is Orthodox, Conservative, or Reform. For example, the Orthodox Jew, much like the Christian, believes that God is spirit, personal, eternal, etc. At the opposite extreme, the Reform

66

Jew is free to believe whatever he or she chooses about God and may even be atheistic.

4. Speak the Gospel with both Testaments. The Old and New Testament together witness to Jesus Christ. Therefore, elements of all of Christianity's basic doctrines can be found in both Testaments.

A. All have sinned and need atonement with God—Ecclesiastes 7:20; Isaiah 64:6; Psalm 14:2–3; Romans 3:23.

B. The result of sin is death—Isaiah 59:1–2; Ezekiel 18:4; Romans 6:23a.

C. God removes sin by sacrifice—Leviticus 17:11; Isaiah 53:3–8; John 1:29; Romans 6:23b.

D. God takes away sin and changes the heart—Psalm 51:7–13; Galatians 2:15–16; 5:22–23.

E. Salvation is received by faith—Genesis 15:6; Galatians 3:6–7.

Be sure to stress the atonement and that Jesus was the final sacrifice for all sin.

5. Learn how Jesus fulfilled the prophecies of the Jewish Bible. It is not appropriate in every conversation to say that Jesus fulfilled the prophecies of the Jewish Bible, but it is important to do it at the right time, especially when a Jewish person becomes interested in

Christianity. At those special times, the Christian witness needs to know some of the prophecies of the coming Messiah and how Jesus fulfilled them. A few of the basic ones are given here; others may be found in reference Bibles. Of course, the entire Old Testament prepared the way for Jesus and points to Him, but these are specific passages.

Old Testament	Prophecy	New Testament
Genesis 3:15	Seed of the woman	Galatians 4:4
Genesis 12:1–3, 7	Covenant of Abraham	Romans 9:4–5
Genesis 49:10	Tribe of Judah	Matthew 1
Deuteronomy 18:15–19	Prophet like Moses	Acts 3:19–23
Isaiah 7:14	Born of a virgin	Matthew 1:18–20
Micah 5:2	Born in Bethlehem	Matthew 2:1–6
Jeremiah 31:31–34	New covenant	Hebrews 8:1–13
Isaiah 53	Death for our forgiveness	Entire crucifixion
Jonah 1:17–2:10	Resurrection	Matthew 12:39–40; 16:4, 21

6. Study the Scriptures. Give your friend a copy of the Holy Bible, especially the New Testament, and encourage him or her to read it. If your friend knows Hebrew, it may be helpful to give him or her a bilingual version of the Scriptures, Hebrew on one side and English, or Spanish, or another language on the opposite page (see "Hebrew Scriptures" in the list of "Resources: Agencies," at the back of this book). If possible, study it together, the two of you alone or in a small group of Christians.

7. Be patient; build a relationship. Moishe Rosen, director of Jews for Jesus, explains the theme of one of their promotions, "Don't Ask," by the following illustration. "Ask a Jewish grandmother, 'Bubba, how do you feel?' and she'll answer, 'Don't ask.' " Rosen suggests she really means, "Please take an interest in my welfare, and if you show some real concern I would like to tell you."[1] All people want others to care about them, to listen to them, even though sometimes they are reluctant to admit it.

Jewish people are no different than other people in this respect. When we witness to Jewish people, they may not respond positively, but they may still be concerned. They may really want to hear more, especially what your faith in Jesus means to you personally and what it does for you. They are usually more eager to hear your testimony than the doctrines of the Church. Remember, to them the "Church" has been their persecutor for centuries. Take time to develop a relationship. Share yourself, and your Jewish friend will be more ready to share and to listen.

8. Pray. Alan prayed for Steve for two years before Steve took the Gospel seriously. Jesus promised to hear our prayers. We know that it is His will that all people be saved, including His ancient people, the Jewish people. Ask God to guide and bless your witness as you speak the Gospel to Jewish people, and then trust that the Holy Spirit will do just that. He arranges opportunities. He opens hearts. He gives us the words to say. He makes the seed of the Gospel germinate and grow.

RESOURCES

ADDITIONAL READING

Lieske, Bruce J. "A Lost Heritage." *Concordia Journal* (May 1976): 104–9. An overview of how Lutherans witnessed to Jewish people from Luther to the present.

Limburg, James, trans. and ed. *Judaism: An Introduction for Christians*. Minneapolis: Augsburg, 1987. Good paperback summary.

Maass, Eliezer. *Stand Firm: A Survival Guide for the New Jewish Believer*. Lansing, IL: American Messianic Fellowship, 1990. A challenging give-and-take between a Jewish person opposed to missions among the Jews and two Jewish believers.

Rosen, Moishe. *Y'shua: The Jewish Way to Say Jesus*. Chicago: Moody, 1982. Good to give to Jewish people who are open to hearing the Gospel.

Rubin, Barry. *You Bring the Bagels, I'll Bring the Gospel: Sharing the Messiah with Your Jewish Neighbor*. Revised Edition. Baltimore, MD: Messianic Jewish Publishers, 1997. A manual for those wanting to share the Messiah with a Jewish friend or neighbor.

Wilch, John R. "The Land and the State of Israel in Prophecy and Fulfillment." *Concordia Journal* (September 1982): 172–78. A review of the major restoration prophecies with a Christological interpretation.

AGENCIES

The Apple of His Eye Mission Society, P.O. Box 6977, St. Louis, MO 63123. www.appleofhiseye.org—A mission society that works with LCMS World Mission in recruiting and training workers in Jewish evangelism and placing them in "Apple of His Eye" ministries.

Chosen People Ministries, 241 East 51st St., New York, NY 10022. www.chosenpeople.org—One of the largest Jewish mission agencies, with centers in many U.S. cities. Originally known as the American Board of Mission to the Jews. Wide variety of tracts, videos, and books.

Good News for Israel, 6408 Minnetonka Blvd., Saint Louis Park, MN 55426. www.gnfi.org—An outgrowth of the Lutheran Zion Society for Israel, founded in 1878. Quarterly newsletter, speakers.

Light for Israel, P.O. Box 80652, Charleston, SC 29416. www.lightforisrael.org—Provides bilingual Scriptures, Hebrew on one side and another language on the other. Also provides free online editions.

Jews for Jesus, 60 Haight St., San Francisco, CA 94102. www.jewsforjesus.org—The largest Jewish evangelism agency, made up primarily of Jewish believers. Mobile singing group, drama group, speakers. Newsletter, CDs, records, tracts.

Lederer/Messianic Jewish Communications, 6120 Day Long Ln., Clarksville, MD 21029. www.messianicjewish.net—Originally a Lutheran ministry, now interdenominational. Excellent literature. Helpful ministry to other Jewish evangelism agencies.

Lutherans in Jewish Evangelism, 6327 Clayton Ave., St. Louis, MO 63139. www.lije.org—A mission society of Missouri

Synod congregations and individuals interested in Jewish evangelism. A Recognized Service Organization of The Lutheran Church—Missouri Synod. Newsletter, presentations, materials, tracts.

NOTES

CHAPTER ONE

1. *American Jewish Yearbook* (New York: American Jewish Committee, 2006).

2. Peter Y. Medding, *The Transformation of American Jewish Politics* (New York: American Jewish Committee, Institute of Human Relations, 1989).

3. Eric W. Gritsch, *Luther and the Jews: Presentations* (New York: Lutheran Council in the USA, 1983), 9.

4. For a more detailed history of Lutherans in mission to Jewish people, see Bruce Lieske, "A Lost Heritage," *Concordia Journal* (May 1976): 104–9.

CHAPTER TWO

1. Mordecai Kaplan, *Judaism as Civilization*, reprint (Philadelphia: Jewish Publication Society, 2010).

2. *St. Louis Post Dispatch*, January 6, 1990, 6D.

CHAPTER THREE

1. Rabbi Hillel Silver, *Where Judaism Differed: An Inquiry into the Distinctiveness of Judaism* (Philadelphia: Jewish Publication Society, 1956).

2. See Fred Skolnik and Michael Berenbaum, *Encyclopedia Judaica* (Detroit: Thomson Gale, 2007).

CHAPTER FOUR

1. Luther, Martin, "That Jesus Christ was Born a Jew," in vol. 45 of *Luther's Works: The Christian in Society II*, ed. Walther I. Brandt (Philadelphia: Fortress, 1962).

CHAPTER FIVE

1. Martin Luther, "On the Jews and Their Lies," in vol. 47 of *Luther's Works: The Christian in Society IV*, ed. Franklin Sherman (Philadelphia: Fortress, 1971), 121–306.

2. The Lutheran Church—Missouri Synod, Resolution 3–09, in *Convention Proceedings* (St. Louis: Concordia, 1983).

CHAPTER SIX

1. The Lutheran Church—Missouri Synod, Resolution 1-30, in *Convention Proceedings* (St. Louis: Concordia, 1979).

CHAPTER SEVEN

1. Moishe Rosen, "Don't Ask," *Jews for Jesus Newsletter*, November 1989

Notes

Notes

Notes

Notes

Notes